A City Street

Kara Stewart

New York

This is my street.

My street has a
police station.

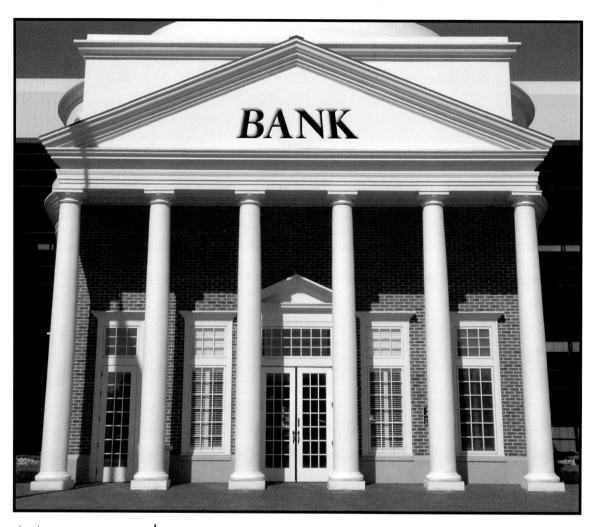

My street has
a bank.

My street has
a store.

My street has
a park too!

My City Street

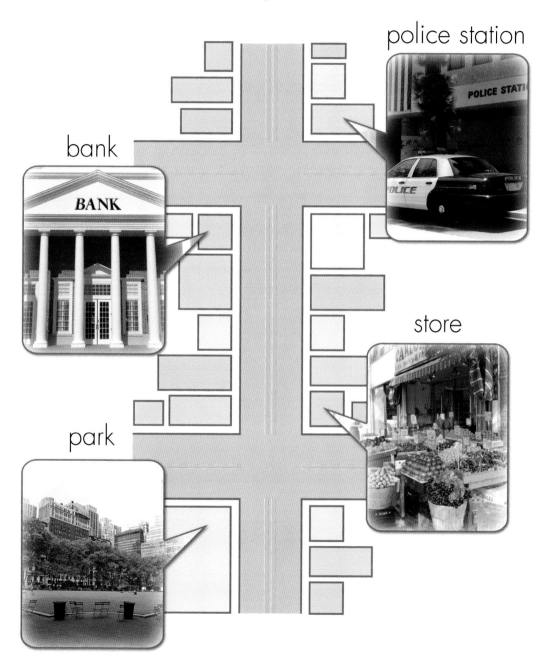

police station

bank

store

park

Words to Know

bank

park

police station

store

street